T0207722

POEMS, PRAYERS, AND REFLECTIONS ON
NATURE, FAITH IN GOD, AND CHRISTMAS

Expressions of the Heart

KATHY PHILLIPS

WESTBOW
PRESS®
A DIVISION OF THOMAS NELSON
& ZONDERVAN

WestBow Press books may be ordered through booksellers or by contacting:

WestBow Press
A Division of Thomas Nelson & Zondervan
1663 Liberty Drive
Bloomington, IN 47403
www.westbowpress.com
1 (866) 928-1240

Scripture taken from the King James Version of the Bible.

ISBN: 978-1-9736-7421-4 (sc)
ISBN: 978-1-9736-7420-7 (hc)
ISBN: 978-1-9736-7422-1 (e)

Library of Congress Control Number: 2019913542

Print information available on the last page.

WestBow Press rev. date: 09/20/2019

Dedication

In memory of Leta B. Denney Nichols
"Mama Nick"
who found poetry in the flight of a butterfly,
the song of a bird,
the smell of a rose—
and who passed her love of poetry, her desire to paint,
and her green thumb along to a very grateful granddaughter;
and
for Brenda Bridges,
who made this book possible.

Contents

Introduction xi

Acknowledgments xiii

Jesus 1

Autumn 2

God Can 3

Dreaming 4

Harvest Moon 5

Fall 6

My God 7

Oh, Lord 8

Dad 9

My Lord 11

A Glimpse of God 12

No Man Hath Seen God 13

Seasonal Gossip 14

A Mother's Task Is Never Done 15

Just Ordinary People 17

Building Children 18

Mornings with God 19

Seek Your Face and Pray 20

A Gift for My Mother 22

The Best Things in Life 24

Images 26

Plans 27

Special People.. 28
Potential.. 29
Certain Kinds of People 30
His Light Divine 31
Gifts.. 32
The Prints You Left Behind 33
Keep My Place in Line 34
My Son 36
What I Would Teach My Son 37
From Boy to Man.. 38
All of God's Tomorrows... 39
Too Many Times 40
God-Given Talents 41
The Pit.. 42
The Master Carpenter 43
Christ's Unbounded Love 44
Friendship 45
Here Within My Heart... 46
A Climb to Destiny... 47
A Battle Well Fought 48
The Steps of God 49
My Friend's Heart 50
Goals... 51
The Careful Gardener 52
The Arms of Jesus 53
What a Wonderful Father Is He 54
There Is Love 55
And All at Once 56
The Good Shepherd... 58
Christmas Proclamations... 60
A Child Is Born... 61
A Christmas Prayer.. 62
Families Make Christmas 63

Christmas *Is* a Child 64

A Texas Christmas 65

Christmas Thanks 66

A Gift for Mom 67

Countdown to Christmas 68

Images of Christmas 69

A Recipe for Christmas Cheer 70

The Sights and Sounds of Christmas 72

Christmas Blessings 74

The Perfect Christmas 76

Seasonal Attire 77

Sing a Song of Christmas 78

Echoes of Christmas 79

The Christmas Party 80

Christmas in My Heart 81

A Quiet Arrival 82

A Dream of Christmas 83

Twelve More Days of Christmas 85

The Point of Christmas 88

Hosanna 90

The Tapestry of Light 92

I Believe in Christmas 94

Home for Christmas 96

It's All about the Light 97

A Christmas Wish 98

Christmas Lights 99

On to Bethlehem 100

The Christmas Spirit 101

The Christmas Cat 103

About the Author 105

Introduction

The poems in this book are divided into two main sections: miscellaneous poems—which contain poems about nature, human relationships, and faith—and Christmas poems. I have included poems that were so easy to write they almost flowed off the tip of the pen, as well as those that were plain hard work. These represent the ups and downs of life and the questions we find ourselves asking as Christians. It is easy to observe the growth and maturity of an author by following the changes in the works they produce over time. For this reason, the poems in each section of this volume are placed in chronological order.

Acknowledgments

I wish to acknowledge with grateful thanks the many people who encouraged me through the years by critiquing, proofing, and editing my poems, as well as those who may recognize themselves as the inspiration for some of the poems I have written. I wish to offer a special thanks to Ginny Lowe for her editorial comments.

Jesus

He came to earth when heaven was much better
To live a life when living was so hard,
Then died a death, a death that wasn't easy,
To rise again and live eternally.

His name is Jesus, Master, Lord, and Savior.
He takes my hand, and through this world we go.
And though sometimes my heart gets tired and heavy,
He's always there to comfort and console.

Autumn

I'm longing for the golden brown that nature sends each year
And for the colors orange and red that in the fall appear.
I'm anxious for the chilly breath that autumn breathes each year
And for the soft and furry coats donned by the squirrel and deer.
This longing that sleeps deep all year and keeps itself so quiet inside
Wells up this season just in time to thrive upon the first hayride.
Not even nature calms my soul when all my heart fills with desire,
And even as I don my coat, my longing soars much higher.
Autumn is alive!

God Can

A poet I may never be, a writer, probably not.
An artist, well, there's just no way; a singer's voice I have not got.
But God can take my simplest rhymes and pen them in the sky.
And He can make my feeblest strokes sing 'cross the page before my
   eyes.

Dreaming

Someday I'm going to draw a sound
And sing a color scheme.
I'll climb an octave up the scale
To photograph a dream.

Harvest Moon

The solitary eye of the harvest moon rises slowly,
Cradled in hay-colored clouds.
Its transparent arms reaching,
Stretching to the corners of its native fields,
Are searching with its lighthouse eye
To find its place in nature's realm.
Pausing quietly to ponder creation
Or man or God or maybe himself
But never finding the answers to his quests,
He moves on.
His silent mourning touches earth
And meets man's eyes in dawn's dew.

Fall

When leaves turn loose their hold on trees
And colors fade away all 'round,
When bears search high and low for lairs
And breezes turn to whipping towns,
When birds fly south and summer flees
And stoves are lit to kill the chill,
When shades are drawn and windows sealed
And coats and scarves are hunted down,
When trick-or-treaters take their toll,
Then fall has come to town.

My God

My God is not a god who lives
In just one church, one special place.
My God is *the* God. He lives where He wills.
His universe mirrors His face.

My God is not limited to gold or to stone
Or faces in ivory and wood.
He's greater in width and height than the sky.
Could you picture that carved in wood?

My God taught the birds how to sing and to fly.
My God taught the fish how to swim.
My God put the clouds and the stars in the sky.
His birds and His bees sing His hymns.

My God gave me eyes to look on His world.
My God gave me ears to hear.
My God gave me speech and a nose and touch.
They help me remember He's near.

When I think of my God, who can end all wars,
Who can stop all the sorrow and pain,
How can a person not see that He lives?
How can they not know His name?

Oh, Lord

Oh, Lord, what would You ask of me?
To spend myself across some sea?
To live my life so others see
Your love that's living here in me?

Oh, Lord, what use are these, my eyes,
But just to help me realize
That You are there if one but tries
To keep one's heart tuned to the skies?

Oh, Lord, what made You give Your Son?
Was it because He's just the One
To get Your plans for man begun?
How it must hurt when He is shunned.

Oh, Lord, I know Your heart must ache
When in vile sin man does partake.
And with each promise to You man makes,
That's one more promise he may break.

Oh, Lord, and yes, You are my Lord,
And I have trusted in Your Word
For I am one who can't afford
Your truths to read and leave ignored.

Dad

A father is a special man on whom a lot depends.
He loves, he guards, he guides, he shares; his family he defends.
He keeps his family safe and sound against all kinds of harm,
And when an arm or leg is hurt, his kiss works like a charm.
A father's hands are big and strong and yet so gentle, too.
The same hands that can lift great loads can tie a small white shoe.
The same big man who braves the world, who works so hard for pay,
Rolls in the grass, gives piggybacks, and makes it fun to play.
A father watches time go by; he sees his children grow.
He blinks his eyes, and training wheels have got them on the go.
He looks away and then looks back; his kids are in their teens.
He ponders on new kinds of slang and old, worn-out blue jeans.
And then his son gets his first car, his daughter, her first date,
And all they seem to do is go and come and go and come in late.
And then his boy or girl's engaged, and then they take their vows,
And all at once his kids are gone, and he's not sure just how.
Then off the kids go on a trip, and now the fun begins
For this time out, it's Grandpa's turn to babysit weekends.
That grandchild takes him back to years when he was young and
    green
And all of life was black and white and shone with polished sheen.
He easily remembers the laughter and the tears
He knew as a father in his children's younger years.
I know a bit about these guys, these fellows we call "Dad."

They're something that we're born with, and personally, I'm glad.
You see, my dad is quite a guy. He always knows just how
To do and say the wisest things that I've heard up till now.
He helped to shape and mold my life when I was still quite small,
And even now, as I've grown up, my dad stands ten feet tall.
If God should let me be a mom, I'll never be as glad
As when I can give my kids the kind of love I got from Dad.

My Lord

Up on His mountaintops, down by His seas,
My Lord stands beside me. From whom shall I flee?
Through the darkest of moments, the most hostile land,
My Lord walks beside me, my hand in His hand.
'Tween the finished day's sunset, the beginning day's morn,
My Lord leads me gently; each dawn, hope is born.
He teaches me patience for my life in His plans
Through great, patient oceans, lapping eternal sands.
It fills me with wonder as I gaze at His skies,
Such awe and such gladness that God gave me eyes.
When doubts will surround me in uncertain days,
My questions are answered through prayers and praise.
God leads me always in the way I should go.
His love is eternal; He's told me it's so.
My Lord's here to guide me in all that I do.
Take His hand in your trials; He'll walk with you, too.

A Glimpse of God

If I had one thing so precious
As a smile from God shed on me,
I'd gladly give up my belonging
Just a glimpse of that smile to see.

If one of my earthly possessions
Could be measured in love and not gold,
I'd gladly cash in on the treasure,
A glimpse of God's love to behold.

No Man Hath Seen God

"No man hath seen God." But is this so?
Rise up early tomorrow, and watch the sun glow.
Keep your ears open wide; hear the song of that bird?
Now tell me that wasn't God's voice you've just heard.
See the green, grassy meadows? The flowers and the trees?
Feel the cool, tickling softness of the quiet passing breeze?
Gaze up at the stars that glow brightly tonight.
Now bow and praise God for the gift of your sight.
"No man hath seen God?" Oh, I can't agree.
When I look upon God's world, He's all that I see.

Seasonal Gossip

She's back in town and what a sight!
Her hair's askew, and her color's bright.
Blew in with the wind in the midst of night.
Think it could be fall?
A scent surrounds her all her own,
Yet she picks up smells where e'er she's gone.
At times she slips in; this time she's blown.
Surely that is fall.
She skipped in at a prankish rate.
You'd think she'd learn a decorous gait,
But she barrels in like she thinks she's late.
Oh yes, that's our fall.
Sometimes you think she'll change for good,
That she'll settle down—as if she would—
But I think it's doubtful she ever could.
Bless her, that's our fall.
One thing I'd like to see her do
Is hang around for a month or two.
Maybe come for summer and see it through.
Then I long for fall.
One wonders where she goes from here,
Where she finds to visit till next year.
Oh dear, she's gone. Winter's chased her clear.
Farewell. That was fall.

A Mother's Task Is Never Done

A mother's task is never done. From breaking dawn to setting sun
Her days are full of boys and girls, of dirty jeans and soft, clean curls.
A mother's arms are always full of each and every kind of tool
To make a child's day full and bright, and fill a young face with
   delight.
A mother's eyes are never still, watching for any tumble or spill,
Keeping the Band-Aids close at hand; her kisses and hugs so much
   in demand.
A mother's voice is strong and sure, a stern command, a quiet cure.
A voice of love and calm assurance, good child-development
   insurance.
A mother's ears hear every sound, from tiptoeing feet on any ground
To a quietly closing front or back door, or a gentle patter on a
   hardwood floor.
A mother's mind is always there, full of new ideas on styling hair
Or how to study math with ease or easiest ways to win spelling bees.
A mother's heart is quickly filled by quiet whispers in faith revealed,
Like "Boys are dumb and not much fun," or "Mom, I'm sure glad
   I'm your son."
A mother's days are full and long, but still she ends the day in song
With a gentle kiss, a quiet good night, a tucked-in bed, and a turned-
   out light.
A mother's life is not her own till her kids grow up and soon are gone,

Till Grandma's arms spread open wide to bring the grandkids safe inside.

Then she's back to hearing every sound, back to picking up toys thrown on the ground,

Back to helping her daughter or son for a mother's task is never done.

Just Ordinary People

Throughout the countless pages of the histories of man
God used ordinary people to fulfill His greatest plans.
Moses tended sheep for years until his destination
Was pointed out to him by God; he was to lead a nation.
David watched his father's flocks, an ordinary thing,
Yet a shepherd boy was destined to become a nation's king.
Mary, just a teenage girl, was chosen as the one
To be the earthly mother of Jesus Christ, God's son.
Joseph was a carpenter, his greatest tool, his hand,
Yet he it was who taught the Lord the things you'd teach a man.
Just ordinary people like those you sit beside
Kept their lives available for God to lead and guide.
And just by being ready to do as is God's will
Just ordinary folks like us could prophecy fulfill.

Building Children

These simple little granny squares will grow in size and number
Until your he or she beneath a gentle blanket slumbers.
They're kind of like a child, you know; they start out small and
  precious
And in a little while they grow to works of love that bless us.
Some blankets take no time at all and, while they may be pretty,
A blanket slowly, caref'ly built is a blanket strong and sturdy.
And so it is as children grow that those just "pieced together"
Can ne'er withstand the winds that blow when life sends stormy
  weather.
But children built with loving hands down life's roughest roads may
  trod
For these are the children of parents who've placed them in the hands
  of God.
For though God's hands built the universe—strong hands that
  forged mountains tall—
We need His hands to build a child for God's hands are gentlest
  of all.

Mornings with God

I've taken to rising up early of late
Though my early's not early to God.
I stumble from bed with sleep still in my eyes
And into our meeting place trod.
Sometimes in the kitchen, sometimes in the den,
Sometimes on the porch in the chill,
With coffee in hand I go to my Lord
And prepare to be quiet and still.
God's already there with the fire glowing strong
As I take my place at His feet.
We talk and we share and then God fills me full
Of His wonderful, soul-quenching meat.
There's a closeness we share in the dim morning light
And for years I was seemingly blind
To the way that a moment at dawn with my Lord
Can comfort an uneasy mind.
Now my days are much better, my life fuller, too,
And it's shared from beginning to end
For I know though my life should be plagued with dark nights
In the morning, I'll be with my Friend.

Seek Your Face and Pray

God,
It's been so very long, it seems, since I've taken time to pray—
Oh, not the mumbled word of "thanks" that I feel bound to say—
But God,
It's weeks since we've discussed a thing in the way that's known to
    friends
And I sometimes ache to stop and kneel, to become close again,
But then the world demands so much that I feel I ought to give
And it seems so hard to pull away, that "separate" life to live.
It shouldn't be that hard, I know, with you standing by my side.
The world should never mean so much if I'm following your guide.
But I think, Lord, that's the problem. When we so seldom talk
I just don't feel the closeness of our once daily walks.
I guess, Lord, what I really mean in a simple, human way
Is I miss the understanding we shared from day to day,
The way You helped me guard my thoughts, the paths You helped
    me choose,
The mountains that You helped me up, the pride You helped me lose,
The times we shared our tears in loss, the victories we've won,
The words that I so thrill to hear when You, *God*, say, "well done."
Lord,
Help me not to soon forget how close we two can be,
The friendship that You offer, the peace You bring to me,
The easy conversations that can pass 'tween us each day

If I'll take time to turn aside, to seek Your face and pray.

"If my people, which are called by my name,
shall humble themselves and pray, and seek my face and turn
from their wicked ways, then will I hear from heaven, and will
forgive their sin, and will heal their land." —II Chronicles 7:14 KJV

A Gift for My Mother

What do you give to a mother
When the world comes to give her her due
And the best things that you have to offer
Are the things that she's first given you?
For a mother spends all her life loving
In a manner devoted and true
And so, through her living example,
She's taught that devotion to you.
And from that devotion comes courage
To stand up for what you hold true
For devotion is really quite worthless
Unless it is costly to you.
From courage you learn understanding
For you see the strength her life's required.
Her strength then breeds determination
To comfort when life's left her tired.
The things that you learn from your mother
Are lessons it takes time to teach.
And, after a mother's done teaching,
Less time of her own's left to reach
The dreams that she had long before you.
They've been quietly given away,
Laid gently aside to allow her
To devotedly love you each day.

So the things that I'll offer my mother
On this day that's especially hers
Aren't the things I'm unable to give her
Like diamonds or mansions or furs.
But the things that she offered so freely
I'll return in each day that life brings:
The strength and devotion, the courage,
The love that my mother's life sings.

The Best Things in Life

"The best things in life are free," folks have said, but I'm not sure I
   really agree

For the best thing that's happened in my life is the salvation God
   gave to me.

Now, sure, it didn't cost me anything. I just reached out and found
   it was there.

But I'm not the One who was nailed to a tree nor sweat drops of
   blood in my prayer.

All that I did for salvation was to give up a life full of wrongs.

But I'm not the One who was beaten or deserted by once-faithful
   throngs.

No, I'm not the person who suffered, the person who hung there
   and died.

Nor am I the Son God deserted on the day that found Christ
   crucified.

But Christ left His place in the Godhead—and He knew all along
   what would be—

That the people who professed to love Him would leave Him to die
   on that tree.

No, salvation doesn't cost money. It doesn't cause physical pain.

You don't have to visit the country or the tomb where the Master
   was lain.

Just remember this next time you hear that the best things in life are free:

It's true only because of the suffering of one man on a rough, splintered tree.

Images

God, as I look at pictures I see here in my mind
I see Your Son, my Savior, a special man so kind.
I see the woman at the well, her life so full of sin.
I see the living water, Christ's face reflected in.
I see the blind and sick and lame as they to Jesus go.
I see their bodies made complete. I watch their faces glow.
I see dead Lazarus arise from a cold, four-day-old grave
And I see tears in Jesus' eyes; life to His friend He gave.
And then I see Christ Jesus alone upon a tree
And countless people standing by and one of them is me.
And none of us so much as lifts a finger to His aid
Though it was for the debts we owed that He alone has paid.
And then I hear my Savior as He prays, God, to You:
"Father, forgive these people. They know not what they do."
Lord, why when Christ has comforted so many folks in need
Did none of us come to His aid, none offer friendly deed?
When He has freely given us our life and health and love
How could we turn our backs on Him who came from Thee above?
So Lord, today please help me touch some soul who has a need
And let them know it is for You that I have done this deed.
And God, though bodies I can't heal, lives I cannot complete,
Let them through kindness I can show their Savior's kindness meet.

Plans

Oh God,
Such things I want to do, such futures that I've planned,
Such power that I wish I knew, such wealth I would command.
But these are plans I've made for me without one thought of you
Though I should listen just to Thee for things that I ought do.
For your plans for my life might be quite different from my own
And I could live and never see the plans for me you've known.
Unless I listen to your voice and take it to my heart
And try to make the proper choice, those plans could fall apart.
And then, quite possibly, I'd be the reason that some other
Should turn aside from walks with thee and I'd have helped my
    brother
To set out on a path in life that we would all regret—
A road of loneliness and strife. Lord, how could I forget
That if I'd listened first to Thee we could have walked together
Hand in hand as it ought to be with Thee into forever?
So Father take my hand this day, give me good life and full
And never let me draw away, no matter how I pull.

Special People

There've been lots of special people
In this life God's given me,
People who have been my friends,
Who've laughed and cried with me,
Folks whose lives were shining bright
When through dark streets I'd trod,
Those whose faith helped pave the way
To highways straight to God,
Fantastic folks who opened doors
To opportunities,
Loving folks who guided
And so encouraged me.
Some knew that they had helped me,
But most were unaware
That just by being faithful
They showed to me they cared.
And to the folks, these gifts from God,
I pledge my loyalty.
Where would I be today, my friend,
Had it not been for thee?

Potential

Each child has the potential to be "someone" when grown
But only if the proper seeds are fed as they are sown.
For, if allowed, the weeds of life will choke out promised flowers
And drink life-giving water God sends in loving showers.
But if, in faith, the gardener works hard to cultivate
With words of understanding and love instead of hate
And prunes where it is proper and feeds when hunger's there,
Then with God's help each child will grow and good fruit surely bear.

Certain Kinds of People

There are certain kinds of people
Who make special kinds of friends,
Whose close association
Brings you special dividends
Like smiles to brighten rainy days
And shoulders firm and ready,
Understanding hands to clasp
To hold you strong and steady.
Such friends are often hard to find
For God's made but a few
Of those certain kinds of people—
The special few like you.

His Light Divine

When I think of Christian living, the way that it should be,
I see a shining, central light aglow for all to see.
That light, of course, is Jesus, who shines in each man's heart
From the moment that they trust Him and choose to live apart.
For Christian lives are sep'rate from those that others lead
And Christian lives are fuller for Christ fulfills all need.
The light out from the center where it's not quite as bright
Is where the human part of man attempts to blend just right
So that the flaws we humans have are caref'ly kept at bay
As we strive toward perfection and to walk the narrow way.
The farther from the light we go, the harder it will get
To keep from stumbling in the dark or falling in sin's pit.
So if we ever strive to keep close to the central shine,
We'll live the life that God expects and share His Light Divine.

Gifts

If I would use the gifts I have in service for my King,
Then I could show the world my love for Him is not something
To be denied, not shut within this joy-filled heart of mine
And through such service to my King would come such peace divine.

The Prints You Left Behind

Father, yet again I've stumbled in my walk with You today;
I got too close to walls of rock that line the narrow way.
Instead of keeping right in step in line with prints You left
I tried to forge a path, my own, too close to jagged clefts.
That's when I stumbled, Father, and fell flat upon my face.
I'm such a fool to try my steps at any but Your pace
For You traveled in a manner so that I could keep in line
If I'd just pay attention to the prints You left behind.

Keep My Place in Line

Sometimes I slip so far away in such a little while
I never seem to hold my place among Your rank and file.
I'll "dedicate" my life anew and for a time all's well.
I'll read my Bible every day, my testimony tell.
But then the fingers of the world give just the slightest tug
And out the back I quietly run while feeling pretty smug.
A Sunday Christian I'll become. "Just for awhile. Who'll know?"
So just to keep my image up, to Sunday school I'll go.
But fewer Sundays see my face inside the church's door
And soon I'm back to just someone who went there some before.
God,
What is it makes me play this game of hide and seek with You
Especially when I know I'll lose the game or sight of You?
For every time I forward move old Satan's standing there
And each jump t'ward You that I make, he slides me back two
      squares.
Then, when I think I'm gone for sure, I'll feel You by my side
And with Your arm about me, Lord, past Satan we will glide.
You listen to apologies and promises I make
And I can see You wondering just how long it will take
Before I'm slipping once again to Satan's waiting arms
And drinking from his evil cup and tasting all his charms.
Lord, how I wish You'd take my hand and never let me go
Nor ever listen to my pleas when I am begging so

34

To once again become a part of Satan's earthly core
Of self-proclaiming "Christians" who find Your way a chore.
God, with Your help I know the road to heaven will improve
Though even for a Christian true that road is never smooth.
But God, if I were counting on Your strength instead of mine
T'would be a whole lot easier to keep my place in line.

My Son

This tiny little person that I'm holding in my arms
With features like his daddy's
And with more than mother's charms,
With watchful and intent blue eyes,
Small fingers reaching for the skies—
Father, thank You for my boy,
My precious bundle of pure joy.

What I Would Teach My Son

These tiny little fingers that close tightly 'round my own
So soon will be the fingers of a man who's fully grown.
And as the years pass quickly by some things he should be taught
To live and learn and use each day just as a grown man ought.
So, Father, help me this one thing teach to my growing son:
That of the goals he may reach for, in truth, there's only one,
To spend each day as You would have, to strive t'ward Your perfection,
To live that others see in him the light of Your reflection.

From Boy to Man

Someday these tiny fingers will have grown in width and length
Until the tasks they handle will be met with adult strength.
By then, these chubby little feet will have grown to walk down roads
That then grown-up broad shoulders will travel with their loads.
And as this little body grows up and so matures,
So heart and mind will follow and so grow strong and pure.
But this will ne'er just happen. The body must be fed.
Likewise, the tender heart and mind must needs be shaped and led
And then the finished product will be a man so tall
And strong and pure and ready to answer when God calls.

All of God's Tomorrows

The morning's light is breaking. The dawn is just begun.
The day is now becoming a very special one
For somewhere on God's earth today a child will bring new life
Into a sick and dying world that's full of sin and strife.
This child may be a pink-cheeked girl or a healthy, husky boy,
Just so their lives as they grow up are filled with love and joy
And lessons taught like "God is love" and "Christ died for all men"
So by the time this child is grown Christ's love will live within.
Then as they strive to do God's will they're building the foundation
For the world of boys and girls to come from each and every nation.
For all of God's tomorrows begin in just this way.
The future is the product of the children born today.

Too Many Times

Too many times we never speak
The words we ought to share,
The words that say to those we love
How much we really care.
Too many times we never show
Through smile or hug or deed
How much we may appreciate
The love of those we need.
Too many times I've missed the chance
To tell you or to show
That you, to me, are very dear
And that I love you so.

God-Given Talents

God gives us different talents,
More to some than others,
But each is used in services
In working with our brothers
Toward a common, Christian goal
Of sharing Christ with men
So we can lead them to Him
And draw them from their sin.
The types of talents vary
But each is used the same
In working for the kingdom
And spreading Jesus' name.

The Pit

I dug a pit, a place to hide from Jesus.
'Twas black as night, so lonesome and so cold.
He lowered His cross into my hole of darkness,
Reached down His Hand, and drew me to His love.
And now my days shine with Jesus' brightness.
The darkest shadows are all but gone.
The hand He offered still holds me tightly.
Praise God, I'm His for His Son shine lights my soul.
Sometimes my skies cloud; at times, life's hard to handle.
Sometimes it rains and, yes, at times it pours
But after rain there'll be the promised rainbow
And life with Christ—Son shine forever more.
When I seem destined to travel shadowed highways
I may be anxious but never really fear
Because my Savior's still holding to me tightly
And it's His Son shine that lights the pathway clear.

The Master Carpenter

As a child, He learned to whittle shapes in different kinds of wood
And then He learned to drive a peg to make a corner good.
He learned to use his father's plane to smooth a splintered face
And make the weakest frame secure by building in a brace.
And when the product was complete, why then, perhaps He'd add
A touch of polish or of wax and then show it to dad.
Then later in His adult life He turned His builder's hand
From working once in lumber to working now in man.
For now, instead of different woods, He used all kinds of men
And none was thought too warped or rough but all could be
     worked in.
He took each single piece of "wood" and judged its width and length
So He could find its weakest spot, then build upon its strength.
With just a touch of weathering here, a tap with the hammer there,
The sturdy piece could help to brace the load the weak would bear.
And then the Carpenter Himself was nailed upon a tree
And all the world did laugh and mock, and yet, we now can see
That just by being "brace" Himself—the Chiefest Cornerstone—
The Master built the greatest church the world has ever known.
And when His church stands before God, our Savior, in His pride,
Can say unto His Father, "Dad, it's for this work I died."

Christ's Unbounded Love

When I take my final human breath,
When my life on earth is done,
When my soul, unconquered e'en in death,
Has its final vict'ry won,
When the earthly farewells fade away
And the angels' praise takes o'er
And complete and total love's displayed
As I step upon God's shore,
When I meet my Savior face to face,
See my mansion built above,
Then I'll realize amazing grace
And know Christ's unbounded love.

Friendship

If you'll give me your fingers, I'll wrap them in mine
And I'll hold them firmly throughout passing time.
If you'll show me your feelings—it's easy to do—
I'll return the favor and share mine with you.
If you'll shed your laughter on my waiting ears
That laughter will echo all down through the years.
If you'll trust me to care for a piece of your heart
I'll hold it, protect it, when we are apart.

Here Within My Heart

You asked if I would give you a place within my heart,
A place that I could keep you when the two of us must part.
You asked if I would give you my version of a smile
And share a tender moment and a touch once in a while.
You asked what I was thinking when I looked into your eyes
But I knew I couldn't tell you for I knew it wasn't wise.
You asked if I'll remember when our pathways have to part.
How could I e'er forget you when you're here within my heart?

A Climb to Destiny

She studied from the foothills the climb she planned to make
And then resolved to finish, whatever it should take.
She knew that family waited along with all her friends
To urge her quietly onward toward the final end.
The path was always climbing. The slopes were always rough.
But till she climbed that mountain life wouldn't hold enough.
The gravel slipped beneath her. The sun beat on her back.
The trail was often narrow. Her pace was never slack.
And then she topped the summit and all the world could see
She was ready for tomorrow and to face her destiny.

A Battle Well Fought

It takes a special woman to do what you have done.
It takes a lot of courage to finish, once begun.
The obstacles you've tackled, the progress that you've made
Are a measure of your triumph o'er what circumstance forbade.
You've fought the battle bravely and tomorrow's sure to tell
That your future's ever brighter for you've fought the battle well.

The Steps of God

I sat out on the step this morn and shivered in the chill
And listened to the purring cat perched on the windowsill.
I watched the dawn steal 'cross the sky in subtle tone and hue
And bring to life the glitter of the spiders webbed in dew.
The squirrels were noisy in their search 'midst leaves of golds and
reds.
The red birds and the birds of blue were calling from their beds.
I heard the timid rustles from the tangled forest floor
And caught the breath of musty growth of leaf and fungus spore.
Then all at once the noises calmed from tree as well as brush
As all the forest settled 'neath a quiet, expectant hush.
The animals all calmly paused as through the woods we heard
The sound of steps upon the leaves, steps not of beast or bird.
I waited quite expectantly to see whose steps could be
Accompanied by such awed hush and naught but gentle breeze.
And then I knew as He passed by whose steps so quietly trod;
I listened with His creatures to the very steps of God.

My Friend's Heart

Were friendship something tangible,
Something seen as well as heard,
Were it something much more solid
Than a smile or thoughtful word,
Were it solid like a shoulder
Or the clasp of loving hand,
Were it firm and soul-specific
And could carry one's own brand,
Were it harder than a diamond,
More precious than mere gold,
Where would we find to keep it,
This friendship that we hold?
Why not split it in two pieces,
Then we each could keep a part
And we'd know that we both carry
A piece of our friend's heart.

Goals

Of all the goals I've worked for while walking on this earth,
The goal that's most inspired me began with my son's birth
For as I held my baby sleeping at my breast
I vowed that as a mother I'd strive to do my best.
To raise a child who's healthy in body, mind, esteem
To me would be the answer to my heart's dearest dream.
A child who knows he's cherished, who's spiritually strong
Can face what life may offer and not give in to wrong.
Of all degrees or honors that I could ever earn
Not one could be equated with how I'd feel to learn
That I had raised one child who was filled with love and health,
A child who knew his value was indeed his greatest wealth.

The Careful Gardener

While working in my garden, I knelt to tend a rose.
The petals of each single bud I held beneath my nose.
The shade of color graded 'cross the petals where they curled
And often differed greatly as the bud became unfurled.
The leaves and buds were dotted with tiny gems of dew
That brought the rainbow's colors and beauty into view.
And as I pruned the branches that were wont to wander wild
It seemed to me that roses should be treated like a child.
With balanced, timely feedings and pruning as they go
A child will tend to run and climb, to flourish as it grows.
And just as roses will respond to water, care, and light
With healthy limbs that have the strength to shun unhealthy blight,
A child who's nurtured with respect and love as they are due
Can greet the world with blossoms that reflect the care they knew.

The Arms of Jesus

The arms of Jesus hold me to the breast of God each day
And even though the world should call, I shall not draw away
For naught can match the comfort, protection, or the peace
That I'll find near the heart of God through all eternity.

He stands so strong before me; I feel His strength surround
This fragile shell I live in where weakness does abound.
But God's strength is so mighty, He crushes every foe
And yet He holds me to Him with the gentle touch I know.

To me, He is the father; to Him, I am the child.
He leads me and He guides me with lessons firm but mild.
For now, I see Him darkly but one day face to face.
On that day I will know the depth of God's unbounded grace.

What a Wonderful Father Is He

I see my Father's love in the birth of each child,
In parents' eyes that meet in their hope and their pride
As families gather near, clasp their hands at their side.
What a wonderful love to see.

I hear my Father's voice in the cry of the gull
Calling on the breeze 'midst the sea's rushing lull,
In the laugh of a child at the gull's soaring wild.
What a wonderful voice to hear.

I feel my Father's touch as the soft evening breeze
Whispers through the grass with the gentlest of ease,
Soft as every hair in the butterfly's wing.
What a wonderful touch to feel.

I see my Father's tears in the eyes of the old
As life has taken even the dearest they hold.
He has shed those same tears as He gave us His Son.
What a wonderful Father is He.

My Father shares His peace through the call of the dove.
He awes me every day with the depth of His love.
He has sent us His Son, shares His love from above.
What a wonderful Father is He.

There Is Love

There is love. There is love
From the Father through the Son from up above.
He will stand right there beside us. With His wisdom He will guide us
Through the plan He has designed for us with love.

There is love. There is love.
All of nature is a mirror of His love.
With His sunrise He will greet us. With His moonrise day will
    leave us
So each star can be His nightlight from above.

There is love. There is love.
All our lives He will surround us with His love.
With His Son He reaches to us. With His Word He teaches to us
How His Spirit will complete us each with love.

There is love. There is love.
Through eternity, He'll cover us with love.
Let the strength that He will lend us fight our battles and defend us
From the things that separate us from His love.

There is love.
Feel His love.
Share His love.

And All at Once

When the Way seems steep and rough
And my day seems way too tough
And my heart is crying out "enough,"
I'll take time to slip away,
Bow my head and quietly pray
And at His feet my burdens I will lay.

And all at once I feel what just that moment brings,
How my unburdened heart can gladly start to sing
And all the hardest tasks become the simplest things
As I pass all my cares to Jesus Christ, my King.

If I sail out on my own,
Leave the shores that I've been shown
And my course is charted but unknown,
When before the winds I'm blown,
Tossed in darkness and alone,
His Light will guide me back to ports I've known.

And all at once I find if I'll approach the throne
And bend my knee to Him, my prideful heart atone,
I'll never find the need to head out on my own
For now I know for sure that Christ will lead me home.

When I search for words of peace
To help those who beg release
From some pain that never seems to cease,
If I concentrate on Him
Words of comfort can begin
To flow from Him through me and on to them.

And all at once I see that moment transform them
As pain-wracked souls or hearts begin to heal within.
I watch the strength return, the peace restored again
As they pass all their hurts to Jesus Christ, the King.

The Good Shepherd

He calls to them softly; they answer in kind.
He speaks to them then of new pastures they'll find,
Of fresh cobble-stoned streams and clear-watered glade
Surrounded by trees for both shelter and shade.
He calls them by name. His sheep know His voice.
They follow His lead and direction by choice.

A stranger may call them—they feel only fear—
They don't trust the stranger to keep their way clear,
To bind up their wounds or watch over their lambs,
Protect them from dangers from creature or man,
To keep them from straying, from wandering lost,
To lead them to safety no matter the cost.

He settles them early as each night draws nigh.
He sings them to sleep under star-laden sky.
His ears listen keenly from even deep sleep
For dangers or mayhem befalling His sheep.
He greets them each morning, a song in His heart.
Not even the darkness can pull them apart.

When summer is over and autumn is come,
The Shepherd sets out on the long journey home.
For many their travels have come to an end;
They've spent their whole journey on earth with their Friend.
The Shepherd has led them to their destiny
And now they're together through eternity.

Christmas Proclamations

The night sky is illumined far brighter than the day.
The star of proclamation shines forth where Jesus lay.
The angels now are singing a chorus from above,
Proclaiming to expectant hearts God's wondrous gift of love.
The shepherds and the wise men at Jesus' feet bow low—
A silent proclamation, a King for all to know.
Throughout the countless ages, through song and word and strife,
The Christ Child's birth proclaims to us the birth into new life.
So set the bells to ringing the songs we long to hear,
Ringing aloud the world around proclaiming Christmas cheer.

A Child Is Born

The night has come to Bethlehem; the stars grow brighter till
In air that's crisp and cool and calm the world is quiet and still,
Expectantly awaiting now angelic-sung goodwill
And peace on earth to all mankind as prophecy's fulfilled.

Hark! Now the trumpets, loud and clear, blast forth in praises strong
And angels' anthems fill the air in notes of love prolonged
Until the star of Bethlehem explodes to light the throng
And men and animals alike kneel to the heavenly song.

For on this night a Child is born—a tiny, dark-haired thing—
The prophesied Emmanuel. "God with us," angels sing
As God sends down to earth His son, His messenger to bring
His hope for all mankind to trust, Christ Jesus, King of Kings.

A Christmas Prayer

God,

For the star that seemed to herald promise of a new and loving Light
upon the earth

And for the night our Savior came to join us—a human child born
of a virgin birth—

Yes, for the angels praising You with chorus and trumpets sounding
loud across the sky,

For shepherds and their awe when they found Jesus, for wise men as
they knelt to God on high,

Yes, Father, for these things we're truly grateful and treasure all the
awe and joy they bring.

But, Father, thank You most of all that Jesus is more to us than just
an earthly king,

For the light that Jesus brought to us that Christmas shines even now
to light the darkest road

And the trials that He suffered as a human somehow help to
strengthen us beneath our load.

So, Father, thank You for the gift of Christmas, for the love it took
to make Your Son a man,

For allowing us the privilege to know Him and to serve Him in the
best way that we can.

Amen.

Families Make Christmas

It's families that bring laughter into a heart that's sad;
It's families sharing happiness and memories they've had.
It's families that make Christmas—at least, they do to me—
Along with virgin births of kings with poor nativities,
Along with God becoming man, with songs that angels sing,
Along with shepherds—wise men, too—it is a family thing.
For Christ was born to family—an humble birth, it's true—
But born to those hand-picked by God His special task to do,
A family filled with faith and love where Christ could grow and live
Surrounded by belief in God and in the strength He'd give.
For God Himself is Father and we His children be.
His arms are always open to draw us to His knee.
So if you must this season spend Christmas far from home
And need a family's comfort when you feel all alone,
Just close your eyes a moment and picture in your mind
Christ's humble, earthly family, the best that God could find.

Christmas Is a Child

For most, a child's excitement this special time of year
Is the best of Christmas pleasure wrapped up in Christmas cheer.
Their eyes can shine so brightly, their laughter ring so clear.
Their giggles and their whispers are like music to the ear.
The wrappings and the tinsel, the blinking, lighted trees
Were tailor-made for children and tailor-made to please.
And even in the oldest, the most worldly and most wise
There are glimpses of the children peeking out of grown-up eyes.
In remembering my childhood I've laughed and, yes, I've smiled.
At Christmas it's so easy for Christmas *is* a Child.

A Texas Christmas

When Santa comes to our house
He's wearing jeans and spurs,
And though we've lots of evergreens
We've few that we'd call firs.
He never has to fight the snow
Or blizzard-level wind,
But if he touches down 'round here
He'll find he's all fogged in.
In houses north of where we live
The heaters may be running,
But when December comes down here,
Why, most are still out sunning.
If folks down here want snow to fall
The weather may well vex us.
It never snows at Christmas here
'Cause we live in south Texas.

Christmas Thanks

The lights are twinkling on the tree; the tinsel's gently swinging.
The presents all are wrapped and placed; the Christmas bells are
    ringing.
The air outside is cold and sharp but inside candles dancing
Give off a warmth that dims the chill, the Christmas glow enhancing.
My son sleeps snugly in his bed with his simple childlike charm
And hopes to be the first to rise and spread the first alarm.
And as I stand and watch him there, hugging a favorite toy,
I silently must thank my God for my healthy, growing boy.
I have to thank Him for our home, that both warm and fed are we
And that we've things like packages and yes, we've a Christmas tree.
I thank Him that we both are well—that we both enjoy good health.
I thank Him for the things we have, all that indicates our wealth.
I thank Him that our family and friends where e'er they be
Can all enjoy the best life gives and I thank Him we're all free.
And I ask Him as I stand here, as I feel Him very near,
To keep us in His love and care throughout all the coming year.

A Gift for Mom

On Christmas Eve I heard a noise and went downstairs and found
   some toys.
A little elf peeked back at me when I looked underneath the tree.
He put his fingers to his lips, then raised a glass and took two sips
Of milk we'd left for Santa Claus! Said he, "It's fine. I know, because
I help old Santa get the toys to all good little girls and boys."
He finished off the cookies, too, and said that it was just his due.
He checked the toys beneath the tree, then smiled at me in elfin glee
And touched the cap upon his head and sent me quietly back to bed.
On Christmas morn, expectantly, I looked once more beneath the
   tree
And had to smile for there, you see, was one marked "Mom" he'd
   left for me.

Countdown to Christmas

The countdown's heady. The clock is ticking.
The deer are ready. Hear their hooves a clicking?
The trees are decked. See the world's lights glow?
The sky's been checked but there's no sign of snow.
Santa's donned his pants, now there's his jacket.
The reindeer prance and make quite a racket.
The sleigh bells jingle. How the red nose glows!
Here comes Kris Kringle. And now there he goes!

Images of Christmas

The images of Christmas are as varied as they're dear:
Of stockings hung from mantels decked with holly and good cheer,
Of mistletoe in doorways, twinkling lights upon the tree,
Of whispers and of giggles and excited shouts of glee,
Of candles burning brightly and scents that fill the air,
Of packages that rattle and some that break—beware!—
Of brand new decorations mixed with some that Grandma had,
Of anxious children's faces, "Was I good enough or bad?"
But the images of Christmas that bring the greatest joy
Are the smiles that light the faces of grown-up, girl, or boy
When a special gift you offer has the power to impart
Such a magic satisfaction that it echoes in the heart.
So let's approach this season keeping this one thing in mind:
Of all the gifts that we can give, it's certain we will find
It's gifts of love that swell the heart and fill the memory
With images of Christmas love and all that it can be.

A Recipe for Christmas Cheer

Take:
   Toys and trains and candy canes, tinsel, lights, and trees,
   Presents wrapped and stockings hung, smells that tempt and tease.
Add:
   Mistletoe and holly wreaths, caroling and snow,
   Frosted windows, icy ways, a reindeer nose to glow.
Blend:
   Cookies shaped like stars and trees, cakes, and pies, and meat,
   Angels crowning Christmas trees and some in flanneled feet
With:
   Kisses 'neath the mistletoe, sleigh bells in the night,
   Stories told around the fire 'midst laughter, warmth, and light.
Stir:
   Puzzles on the tabletops, games and shouts of glee,
   Presents wrapped behind closed doors and slipped beneath the tree
With:
   Absent friends and family, cards, long-distance calls,
   Stars that glimmer in dark skies, love that decks the halls.

Add:

> Baby Jesus, shepherds, stars, angels heralding,
> Oxen, sheep, nativities, Church bells as they ring.

Bake:

> At friendly temperatures in hearts warmed this time of year
> With memories of love and peace, and you've got Christmas cheer.

The Sights and Sounds of Christmas

Parades and fireworks fill the air with loud and joyous noise
And pots and kettles simmer with the smells a cook employs
While stores and malls are ceiling-high with all the latest toys
And Santa's lap is tired and sore from countless girls and boys
Who climbed aboard and gladly begged for Christmas gifts and joys.

But once the angels filled the air with loud and joyous sound.
The smells of hay, manure, and fur were all that could be found.
The stalls and floor were covered with cut hay thrown on the ground
When a weary little donkey finally reached where he was bound
And the King was born to Mary with His kingdom all around.

Have we failed our children when they see this time of year
As punishment for failure or reward for coming near
To the standards of obedience that their parents hold so dear?
What of giving 'stead of getting? What of peace and love and cheer?
We parents are the ones to help our children keep things clear.

If we don't teach our children the true Christmas sights and joys,
If we don't instill the *Christ*mas in all our girls and boys,
Then who will teach their children when the stores are full of noise
That the season's more than getting all the latest of the toys
Or all the name-brand got-to-haves the retail world employs?

So as we face this season of such sound and smell and sight
Let's focus our attention on that one historic night
When angels brought the message decked in such celestial light
That it led the simple and the great to lay the gifts they might
At the feet of God's own holy Child who woke the world to Light.

Christmas Blessings

I reached high upon a shelf to pull a large box down
And as I reached I paused and then continued with a frown.
And, frowning still, I raised the lid, admitting to myself
That I've been keeping "Christmas" in a box upon a shelf.

The lights, the star, the ropes of color all looked back at me,
The angels, stockings, bows—and, yes, the carved nativity.
All these are things that we might call a Christmas kind of "gear,"
The kinds of things we would expect to store away each year.

But nestled 'neath and wrapped around the holiday's attire
I found some things I had not meant to annually retire.
There sat the joy of giving to those who have real need
And next to it was nestled the peace from such a deed.

Old childlike expectations were all tangled up in lights
And stockings held the memories of family delights.
Chuckles of excitement were found resting next to awe
As I unwrapped the Child so gently cradled in the straw.

Hope embraced a shining star; the kings were wrapped in grace.
The Family was layered between love and peace and lace.
Faith was used as padding for the fragile and the old.
Charity was all used up protecting things of gold.

Laid out there before me were the gifts that make life dear—
It's no wonder I look forward to Christmastime all year.
So this year as I deck the halls I think that there will be
A better understanding of what Christmas means to me.

And when it's time to pack it up and put it all away
I'm going to use a smaller box and pack it all in hay.
That way I'll know that packed inside are only Christmas "things"
And I'll keep out the blessings that Christmas often brings.

The Perfect Christmas

There has to be a foot of snow, lights 'cross the porch, and mistletoe.

The fire must flame up warm and glow. Each package must be wrapped just so.

The candles should be burning bright, the tree alive with twinkling light,

The background music? "Silent Night," each decoration placed just right.

The kettles should boil merrily. The children *must* play happily.

A lovely angel we should see atop the perfect Christmas tree.

But take away the foot of snow, the tinsel, lights, and mistletoe.

Change the hearth to a campfire's glow. Remove the holly and each bow.

Exchange each twinkling little light for stars that twinkle just as bright

And watch your perfect Christmas sight become the perfect silent night.

No matter how we deck our hall we really can't compete at all.

The perfect Christmas, you'll recall, God held within a donkey's stall.

Seasonal Attire

This year I was determined, as the season came along,
To create the kind of Christmas that we celebrate in song.
So I dressed the tree with tiny drums and small red violins
And added polished horns of brass and soldiers made of tin.
I draped the mantle and the stairs with garlands made of green
And tied them up with bright red bows of ribbon in between.
The tabletops were polished to a lemon-oil glow
And doorways shyly sported dangling sprigs of mistletoe.
The angel perched atop her tree and smiled on twinkling light.
The frosted windows shed their warmth upon the starlit night.
The cat was purring softly where it dozed before the fire—
I thought my halls decked properly in seasonal attire.
But as I looked beneath the tree where all the gifts were piled
I noticed something missing—'twas the manger and the Child.
They'd always nestled center stage beneath the boughs of green
But, somehow, they'd been shoved aside, no longer could be seen.
I dug beneath the presents, each adorned with fancy bow,
And found the scattered Family where they'd toppled to and fro,
Then gently set each person 'round the cradle in their place
And focused their attention on the Child's angelic face.
I vowed that in the future I would never be inclined
To deck the halls so splendidly that Christmastime would find
I'd planned the perfect picture for everyone to see
While blotting out the presence of the whole nativity.

Sing a Song of Christmas

Sing a song of Christmas, mistletoe, and snow.
Sing a song of starlight, candles as they glow.
Sing a song of holly, berry, bough, and bow.
Sing a song of Christmas angels bending, oh so low.
Sing a song of children perched upon red knees.
Sing a song of wanting everything one sees.
Sing a song of parents reminding to say "please."
Sing a song of Santa bringing happiness to these.
Sing a song of tinsel, trees of twinkling light.
Sing a song of stars that shine from heaven's height.
Sing a song of choirs singing "Silent Night."
Sing a song of villages all decked in winter white.
Sing a song of mangers, cradles bearing kings.
Sing a song of wise men bringing special things.
Sing a song of shepherds searching for their King.
Sing a song of Christmas angels—hark to how they sing.
Sing a song of warmth for those who have no home.
Sing a song of plenty, so everyone has some.
Sing a song of welcome to the Father's Son.
Sing a song of Christmas Day. God bless us every one.

Echoes of Christmas

Reindeer galloping in the night on their yearly Christmas flight;
Snowflakes falling from the sky with a silent, weightless sigh;
Silver, brass, and golden bells; angels singing first noels;
Fireplace crackles, stories told; children laughing in the cold;
Sleigh bells ringing in the air; Grandpa snoring in his chair;
Smacking 'neath the mistletoe; fa la la la la and ho, ho, ho;
Winds that whistle through the crack; Santa's gifts pulled from a
 sack;
Noses sniffing tempting smells; Christmas glories old folks tell;
Presents rattled 'neath the tree—wonder what that gift can be?—
Choirs singing "Silent Night;" organs played by candlelight;
Cattle lowing from a stall; a Family nestled in the straw;
Cooing of the mourning dove; lullabies sung soft with love;
Rustles in a Baby's sleep; abiding peace for us to keep.

The Christmas Party

The wise men brought their gifts of old: their frankincense and
   myrrh and gold
And laid them at the Baby's feet—a King the very stars would greet.
The angels brought their gift in song; the shepherds brought their
   awe along.
The stable beasts struck up a hum; the little drummer played his
   drum.
The stars sent down their gift of light; the wind's song whispered
   through the night.
The gifts that welcomed Christ to earth—all brought to celebrate
   His birth—
Were gifts that each brought to impart the joy that filled the whole
   world's heart
As God brought forth within a stall the greatest Christmas gift of all.

Christmas in My Heart

Each year I plan a Christmas even better than before
With added decorations, brighter lights around the door,
And presents tailor-made to thrill each person to the core.
It brings childlike excitement, makes my Christmas spirit soar.

But this year I can't decorate the way I always do
With holly decked around the door and lights of green or blue,
No six-foot tree with blinking lights that sparkle like fresh dew,
Few candles lit with dancing flames of soft and golden hue.

One large red bow, no mistletoe, few ornaments displayed,
No strings of beads or tinsel, some Christmas carols played,
No fudge or bread or casseroles, no cookies will be made.
But yes, there'll be a manger where the Baby will be laid.

We can't be all together—we'll be short some family.
We won't share Christmas dinner or our gifts as happily.
I'll miss my son's expression as he peaks inside to see
If mom "came through" this Christmas with the gift beneath his
    tree.

Still, in my heart it's Christmas. I close my eyes and find
That all the single scenes I've stored have merged and so combined
To sum up all my memories. That total has defined
The whole that is the Christmas that is here within my mind.

A Quiet Arrival

Close your eyes a moment. Now pause within your mind.
Think back through the centuries to what you'll likely find.
The breeze is sharp and chilling; the stars are huge and bright.
The roads are far more traveled than is usual for night.
No matter where they query, there is no place to stay.
Every inn they stop at sadly turns them both away
Until they find a keeper who shrugs and lets them stay
With their donkey in a stable of freshly layered hay.
For years the world has waited for the King that she will bear
And yet the world has not a clue that He is born right there
In a pile of straw that most would use to cast upon the floor.
They never dream a manger could be used for something more
Than a trough to feed the cattle or the gently snoring sheep
Who witness God-turned-into-man as He lay sound asleep.
Because the world was looking in the places they "should" see
The birth of One they knew would change the course of history
They missed the quiet arrival of the very Child they sought
And few have learned the lesson that His birth was to have taught.
Our human expectations rarely lead to all the joy
That God passed proudly to us with the birth of that one Boy.

A Dream of Christmas

I finished an exhausting day with late news on the screen
And knew I'd probably dream of all the horrors I had seen.
I wasn't really anxious to close my eyes in sleep
Because my mind so seldom sinks into that restful deep.
But I dreamed a dream of Christmas, of loved ones home from war.
I dreamed a world where fighting never happens anymore.
I dreamed a dream of family drawn close from far apart.
I dreamed of love that holds us each as close as our own heart.
I dreamed a world of friendship where no one is alone,
Where "lonely" has no meaning—it isn't even known.
I dreamed a dream of giving to those who are in need.
I dreamed of sharing laughter so that broken hearts are freed.
I dreamed a world of plenty where no one is without;
"Enough" is something each one has. There's never any drought.
I dreamed of bringing warmth to those who suffer in the cold.
I dreamed of youth returning to the prematurely old.
I dreamed a dream of Christmas, of candlelight and stars,
Of carols sung around the tree or hummed as quiet bars.
I dreamed of winds that whisper as they tiptoe through the night,
Of kings who follow stars that flood the world with holy light,
Of shepherds who go searching for a birth foretold in song,
Of angels heralding the news that Christ has come along.
I dreamed a dream of Christmas but feared I'd wake to find
The world would still be much the same as I had left behind.

But that's what dreams are all about—the way the world should be,
The kind of place we'd want to live and have our children see.
I dreamed a dream of Christmas then woke expectantly
Believing Christmas dreams come true, with help from you and me.

Twelve More Days of Christmas

Every year at Christmas, I turn my 6-foot, artificial, bought-after-Christmas-on-sale tree into an absolutely gorgeous work of art. With strings of cream-colored beads and gold and brass and glass and red ornaments and small white lights, I transform a fake tree into a tree fit for royalty. Of course, the only ones who usually see it are the resident cats and an occasional stray relative or friend. There is a period of adjustment (mostly mine) with each new cat that passes through the family. After all, it *is* a tree and they *are* cats and cats are gonna do what cats are gonna do with trees. With the loss of my old friend Tigger (who climbed the Christmas tree once and used up one of his lives when it fell and scared him nearly to death) and the entrance of the two mostly wild strays born under a neighbor's trailer, we've had to start the process all over again. These two, Bubba and Felicia, have inspired this year's Christmas offering to my friends and family. Not only is it impossible not to climb the tree and dislodge as many branches as possible, but it is evidently a requirement that with each subsequent climb you must bring down more ornaments than the last time around. By the end of any given day, there is usually quite a collection of dislocated ornaments and dismembered limbs at the base of the tree. You may be certain that Bubba and Felicia are quite proud to have inspired the following—which is, of course, to be sung to the tune of the Twelve Days of Christmas. (I dare you.)

On the first day of Christmas my kittens brought to me the angel from atop the Christmas tree.

85

On the second day of Christmas my kittens brought to me two crystal snowflakes and the angel from atop the Christmas tree.

On the third day of Christmas my kittens brought to me three ceramic kitties, two crystal snowflakes, and the angel from atop the Christmas tree.

On the fourth day of Christmas my kittens brought to me four strands of beads, three ceramic kitties, two crystal snowflakes, and the angel from atop the Christmas tree.

On the fifth day of Christmas my kittens brought to me five golden bells, four strands of beads, three ceramic kitties, two crystal snowflakes, and the angel from atop the Christmas tree.

On the sixth day of Christmas my kittens brought to me six satin bows, five golden bells, four strands of beads, three ceramic kitties, two crystal snowflakes, and the angel from atop the Christmas tree.

On the seventh day of Christmas my kittens brought to me seven strings of lights, six satin bows, five golden bells, four strands of beads, three ceramic kitties, two crystal snowflakes, and the angel from atop the Christmas tree.

On the eight day of Christmas my kittens brought to me eight small brass horns, seven strings of lights, six satin bows, five golden bells, four strands of beads, three ceramic kitties, two crystal snowflakes, and the angel from atop the Christmas tree.

On the ninth day of Christmas my kittens brought to me nine large gold drums, eight small brass horns, seven strings of lights, six satin bows, five golden bells, four strands of beads, three ceramic kitties, two crystal snowflakes, and the angel from atop the Christmas tree.

On the tenth day of Christmas my kittens brought to me ten red violins, nine large gold drums, eight small brass horns, seven strings of lights, six satin bows, five golden bells, four strands of beads, three ceramic kitties, two crystal snowflakes, and the angel from atop the Christmas tree.

On the eleventh day of Christmas my kittens brought to me eleven clear glass angels, ten red violins, nine large gold drums, eight small brass horns, seven strings of lights, six satin bows, five golden bells, four strands of beads, three ceramic kitties, two crystal snowflakes, and the angel from atop the Christmas tree.

On the twelfth day of Christmas my kittens brought to me twelve bright red apples, eleven clear glass angels, ten red violins, nine large gold drums, eight small brass horns, seven strings of lights, six satin bows, five golden bells, four strands of beads, three ceramic kitties, two crystal snowflakes, and the angel from atop the Christmas tree.

The Point of Christmas

If we face the Christmas season with a shudder of real dread
And the thought of so much family brings a pounding to our head,
If we cringe at just the thought of buying presents for them all
And we can't imagine anything could drag us to the mall,
If we worry over whether all the neighbors will spend more
On their outside decorations or the wreaths upon their door,
We've missed the point of Christmas.

If we plan a Christmas menu that will fill us till we moan
And never once give thought to those whose hunger makes them
  groan,
If our houses are well lighted and we're warmed against the cold
But forget about the homeless, the lonely, and the old,
If we spend so much at Christmas that we pay it off each year
With not a thought for those to whom a single gift is dear,
We've missed the point of Christmas.

If we deck our halls in splendor and ourselves in new attire
And we party in the workplace and at home around the fire,
If we focus our attentions on the glitter and the fun
And never for a moment do we focus on the One
Whose birth began this season many centuries in the past,
Whose love instills a reason, a hope, a peace that lasts,
We've missed the point of Christmas.

If we'd once been in attendance at the coming of the King,
If we'd seen the star of Bethlehem or heard the angels sing,
If we'd witnessed shepherds coming in their awe and maybe fear
And watched the caravan approach as foreign kings drew near,
If we'd been at His nativity and watched the whole world greet
The Son sent from the Father and we'd worshiped at His feet,
We'd know the point of Christmas.

Hosanna

The night was dark; the air was chill. The stars were bright, one
   brighter still.
It led the way across the hills to bring them both to here.
They couldn't find a place to stay. Each query had them turned away
Till they found a stable filled with hay to lay their weary heads.

Hosanna, hark now the angels sing.
Hosanna, He is the King of kings.
Hosanna, Hosanna, His star will light the way to Him.

The shepherds in the hills that night beheld the star of such great
   light.
In fear they bowed before the sight that heralded His birth.
The star led them to where He stay—a manger freshly lined with hay.
They knelt before Him as He lay, in awe before a King.

Hosanna, hark now the angels sing.
Hosanna, He is the King of kings.
Hosanna, Hosanna, His star will light the way to Him.

The wise men studied from afar. They traveled long. They traveled far.
They had to reach the distant star—they knew what they would find.
They brought myrrh, frankincense, and gold, gifts for the Child the
   star foretold.
They knelt before Him to behold Christ Jesus, King of Kings.

Hosanna, hark now the angels sing.
Hosanna, He is the King of kings.
Hosanna, Hosanna, His star will light the way to Him.

His star will light the way to Him. His star will light the way to Him.
HOSANNA!

The Tapestry of Light

The story of Christmas is a story of Light. The Light that was promised from the beginning of time, who was revealed when the world needed Him most. It was light that the wise men followed mile after mile in search of the newborn King. It was a host of angels in a heaven filled with light who told of the coming of Jesus. The Light was part of the story before man even knew there would be a story. It was only revealed when the time was right and the world was ready. It was part of the Master Designer's story, unfolded as He chose to tell it, almost like a painting, a mural, or perhaps, a tapestry.

Our lives are but a portion of a master tapestry;
The threads wind through the decades as they weave our destiny.
Each pattern, once begun, will make a statement of its scheme
And hopefully blend seamlessly into the Weaver's theme.
Some common threads are woven throughout countless generations—
Threads focused more on faith and love and less on human nations,
Threads of wisdom, strength, and peace, equality and Light,
Threads with hints of golden hues to keep the portrait bright
Enough to thrust the picture from a background dark and grayed
Into a foreground filled with white and palest hues displayed.
True White is often veiled within the tapestry of life—
The darkest shades outstrip it with tempest and with strife.
And though the Light is present in every passing scene,
The human eye oft' misses it without its golden sheen.
I think that's why the Weaver in His wisdom of design

Foresaw the need to weave the Light through neverending lines
Begun before the clock began to tick away the years
Until the Light burst from the dark unveiled by Mary's tears.
The shepherds and the wise men are woven on their knees,
Their gifts laid out before them in hopes that they will please
The Child with shining halo worked in threads of gold and white—
His debut in the Weaver's finest tapestry of Light.

Our portrait will be up to us for we are weavers, too.
We'll weave the threads both dark and Light however we will choose
Until our lives are but a scene in the tapestry become
The Master's greatest story since the world was e'er begun.

I Believe in Christmas

Though I've never seen eight reindeer prancing on my roof
Or elves along as helpers to act as any proof
And I've never peeked at Santa decked out in white and red
Or dreamed of things like sugar plums when I lay down in bed,
I believe in Christmas.

I may not get as presents each thing that I wish for.
I may be missing holly boughs hanging on my door.
My tree may not be bigger than any other tree.
My lights could still be brighter for everyone to see
That I believe in Christmas.

See, I *believe* the tale of a Babe in swaddling clothes
And I can *see* the details that everybody knows:
The donkey ride to Bethlehem, the search to find a room
To rest and birth the Baby that she carried in her womb.
Oh, I believe in Christmas.

I even hear the choirs that filled the starlit night;
I sense the awe of shepherds drawn closer to the sight.
I've seen the star of Bethlehem enormous in the sky
And watched the wise men coming as the star drew closer by.
Sure, I believe in Christmas.

Christmas isn't just a day we celebrate each year.
It's not just decorations or holidays of cheer.
It's the tiny little Baby that God sent from above
To lead us to the Father through His Christmas gift of love.
Yes, I believe in Christmas.

Home for Christmas

No matter where I wander, it seems to me I find
A single destination often lingers in my mind:
The place I carry with me as I travel through my way,
The place my heart has longed for nearly every passing day.

The place where once I dared to dream the dreams t'would take
　　me far,
The place reserved for "just in case" those dreams should fall apart,
The place that calls me back when my path has urged me on,
A smell, a something in the air that always triggers "home."

This year, I'm spending Christmas in my corner of the globe,
A place with trees I planted over twenty years ago,
A place where deer and squirrel roam free, where wind blows as it
　　roams,
Where rain is echoed in each tree—the place for me that's "home."

So this, my favorite season, in my favorite place on earth
Will be a celebration—not just of my Savior's birth—
But a coming home to family, to scents of woods and pine,
A welcome back to all the things that make this corner mine.

Merry Christmas

It's All about the Light

My angel sits atop her tree 'midst boughs of decked-out green
And views the world she looks upon through white and shining
   sheen.
The boughs are lit with lights of white revealing 'tween the limbs
The sparkle of red, white, and gold that glistens just like gems.
The tree without the lights would be an ordinary sight
But add a string or two of bulbs?—it springs alive with light.
It's all about the light.

Without the light the sun provides, the world could not survive.
We'd not have plants or food to eat—we wouldn't be alive.
The moon could not provide our light for it can just return
The light the sun shines on the earth. The moon, it does not burn.
The brightest stars within the sky cannot produce the light
That's needed for a man afoot to travel through the night.
It's all about the light.

But once the darkest sky was lit by rare celestial light,
So even those who traveled far could see throughout the night.
This light was from the brightest star the naked eye has seen
And led the shepherds and the wise to find an infant king,
A king born into darkness in the squalor of a stall
Where God passed proudly to us the greatest Light of all.
It's all about the Light.

A Christmas Wish

Now I lay me down to sleep. I pray that sleep is long and deep.
And when I next should see the sun, I hope the dishes will be done.
I pray the elves will come tonight and clean my home with all their
    might.
And for those gifts I need to wrap, I'll close my eyes and simply clap,
Then open wide to foil and bows beneath a tree that simply glows
With sparkle, glitter, crystal, light, and background music—"Silent
    Night."
I'll place the carved nativity 'neath the boughs of the Christmas tree,
Then settle back to watch TV while folks chow down on H.E.B.

Christmas Lights

Twinkle, twinkle little lights, twinkling on this night of nights,
Twinkling from both tree and sky, from home and buildings oh, so
   high,
Twinkling down through air so cold, twinkling during stories told,
Twinkling 'cross the mantles dressed, down banisters with bows
   fresh-pressed.
Twinkle as you did on Them, on their trip to Bethlehem
When you twinkled through the birth that brought Peace to man
   on earth.
Twinkle brightly, twinkle clear, twinkle in a bright new year.

On to Bethlehem

To Bethlehem they traveled from a Galilean town,
Returning to his tribal home for taxing by the crown.
Their journey was not easy for they traveled rocky earth,
But they reached their destination in time for Jesus' birth.

To Bethlehem they traveled from the heavens up above,
Proclaiming to all men below the birth of living Love.
They filled the sky above the earth with presence and with sound
And heralded His coming throughout field and all around.

To Bethlehem they traveled from their flocks out in the fields,
Searching for the newborn Child the angels had revealed.
They left their flocks in pastures that were bathed in holy light
To find the babe that Mary brought into the world that night.

To Bethlehem they traveled from their kingdoms 'cross the sand,
Following the star-filled sky that led them to His land.
They brought Him gifts of frankincense, of myrrh, and, yes, of gold
And worshiped at the feet of One the prophets had foretold.

To Bethlehem I travel every Christmas in my mind
To celebrate the birth of Christ and pray that *you* will find
The joy and peace, the hope and love our Savior has to share
With all who come to celebrate. I hope to see you there.

The Christmas Spirit

I lost my Christmas spirit, couldn't find it anywhere.
I searched in tubs and boxes, under couch and easy chair.
I excavated closets, went through my boxed-up tree.
I couldn't find a sliver of Christmas joy or glee.
I didn't find it shopping while online or at the mall
And not a single catalog sold "peace on earth to all."
But, while I was out searching, I found a barefoot child.
His feet were cold and dirty and the weather wasn't mild.
I took him to a shelter where we washed his calloused feet,
Then bought him shoes, a set of clothes, so he'd be warm and neat.
I thought that I could leave him there because I'd done my due,
But when I looked into his eyes I knew it wasn't true.
He needed food, clean water, the safety of a home,
The chance to grow, to learn—he'd never find those on his own.
The shelter housed a homeless man who couldn't pay his rent;
He and his wife and children had been sleeping in a tent.
He'd lost his job, the bills piled up, his wife was very ill;
He'd searched the city over looking for a job to fill
His pockets with the money to get his wife some care
But so far all he'd found was a room that they could share.
All he wanted was the chance to care for his family,
To give them back the life they'd lost—get back their hope, you see.
It took awhile to understand how selfish I could be,
My focus only on myself left little room to see

The needs of those less fortunate that I found everywhere
Could easily be satisfied if I'd take time to share
The things I take for granted because they're always there—
A home, good friends, and family, a cupboard never bare.
And then I understood my Christmas spirit wasn't gone;
It just had been neglected by the little I had done
To keep it happy, healthy throughout each passing day
By helping those I find in need as I go on my way.

"And the King shall answer and say unto them, Verily I say unto you, Inasmuch as ye have done it unto one of the least of these my brethren, ye have done it unto me." —Matthew 25:40 KJV

The Christmas Cat

Legend has it that a tabby kitten curled up next to the shivering newborn Jesus to keep Him warm all night. In return, Mary left her mark—an "M"—on the kitten's head in gratefulness for its kindness. This mark has been passed down through the ages on each tabby born since that time. This is my version of how that night may have played out.

They stumbled in bone weary—the woman great with child.
The donkey stuttered to a stop; the father's grunt was mild.
The inn the keeper kept was full but he said that they could stay
In the stable with the cattle in freshly layered hay.

I watched them settle in for night; I watched the child be born.
The babe was swaddled tightly to try to keep him warm.
They laid him in a manger to keep him off the floor,
Away from drafts that quietly tiptoed underneath the door.

The parents were exhausted and settled in to sleep
But were to be awakened by shepherds keeping sheep
Come to find the child proclaimed by angels from above
As the king long awaited to rule the world with love.

The guests awoke the child, who could not go back to sleep,
And as the babe was fretful the cold began to seep
Along the cobbled floor from the door thrown open wide
As the shepherds told their tale of angelic hosts outside.

Mary watched the child with worry penciled on her brow
And hoped the boy was warm and could get back to sleep somehow.
I climbed down from my hiding place and tiptoed to his side.
She saw me as I broached the child—her eyes were opened wide.

I slipped into the manger and curled up by the boy.
My quiet purring soothed him, which filled my heart with joy.
The fretful child soon warmed and went quietly back to sleep.
Joseph watched the pair till his sleep was quiet and deep.

The babe awoke at dawn with me curled against his side.
When Mary checked the child she found his eyes were open wide.
She stroked my forehead softly and thanked me for my care
And left her mark—an "M"—on my forehead in my hair.

Throughout the countless ages of history since that eve
Each tabby cat is born with a mark like I received,
A mark to remind us to give all that we can spare
To each one we encounter, our Christmas spirit share.

About the Author

Kathy Phillips has been writing poetry since the sixth grade. Her original files contain "scribbles" on napkins, envelopes, and the backs of church bulletins, depending on where she was when words came to her. Her poetry has been published in newspapers and both high-school and national anthologies. Ms. Phillips lives in the woods outside of Huntsville, Texas, with her two cats and assorted wildlife.

Printed in the United States
By Bookmasters